HISTORY IN LITERATURE

THE STORY BEHIND...

MARK TWAIN'S
ADVENTURES OF HUCKLEBERRY FINN

Rebecca Vickers

Heinemann
LIBRARY

www.heinemann.co.uk/library
Visit our website to find out more information about Heinemann Library books.

To order:
 Phone 44 (0) 1865 888066
 Send a fax to 44 (0) 1865 314091
Visit the Heinemann Bookshop at www.heinemann.co.uk/library to browse our catalogue and order online.

First published in Great Britain by
Heinemann Library, Halley Court, Jordan Hill,
Oxford, OX2 8EJ, part of Harcourt Education.
Heinemann is a registered trademark of
Harcourt Education Ltd.

© Harcourt Education Ltd 2007

Editorial: Louise Galpine, Lucy Beevor,
    and Rosie Gordon
Design: Richard Parker and
    Tinstar Design
Maps: International Mapping
Picture Research: Melissa Allison
Production: Camilla Crask
Originated by Modern Age
Printed and bound in China by Leo
Paper Group

10 digit ISBN 0 431 08171 9
13 digit ISBN 978 0 341 08171 7

11 10 09 08 07
10 9 8 7 6 5 4 3 2 1

British Library Cataloguing in Publication Data
Vickers, Rebecca
The story behind Adventures of Huckleberry Finn.
- (History in literature)
    I.Title
    813.4
A full catalogue record for this book is available
from the British Library.

Acknowledgements
The publishers would like to thank the
following for permission to reproduce
photographs/ quotes: **p. 41**, Bridgeman Art Library/
Wilberforce House, Hull City Museums and Art
Galleries, UK; **p. 21** thumbnail, Buffalo and Erie
County Library; **p. 31**, Corbis; **pp. 7, 9, 11, 12,
13, 36, 39, 45, 47, 33, 40** Corbis/Bettmann; **p.
44**, Corbis/Metropolitan Museum of Art NYC; **p.
29**, Corbis/Swim Ink 2, LLC; **p. 34**, Corbis/ Zefa/
Wolfgang Flamisch; **p. 19**, Courtesy the Mark Twain
Archive, Elmira College; **p. 49**, Getty Images/Time
Life Pictures; **pp. 23, 27, 32** Getty/Hulton Archive;
pp. 14, 43. Library of Congress; **p. 22**, Library of
Congress/ Frances Benjamin Johnston Collection;
pp. 5, 18, 24, 25, 35, 37, 42, 46, 28, Mark Twain
Boyhood Home Museum; **pp.16, 38**, Mary Evans
Picture Library; **p. 8**, Museum of American
History, Smithsonian Institute; **p. 48**, The Kobal
Collection/Walt Disney Pictures; **pp. 4,10, 15, 17,
26**, The Mark Twain Project, The Bancroft Library;
p. 21 middle, Ulster Museum, Belfast/ Photograph
reproduced with the kind permission of the Trustees
of the National Museums Northern Ireland. **Cover**:
Corbis/Bettmann.

P49 1) Extract from Green Hills of Africa by
Ernest Hemingway published by Jonathan Cape,
with permission of The Random House Group. 2)
Reprinted with permission of Scribner, an imprint of
Simon and Schuster Adult Publishing Group, from
Green Hills of Africa by Ernest Hemingway. © 1935
by Charles Scribner's Sons. © renewed 1963 by
Mary Hemingway

The publisher would like to thank Megan Rapp for
her assistance in the preparation of this book.

Contents

Sam Clemens of Hannibal, Missouri 4

The wider world beckons 8

A nation divided against itself 12

Mr Mark Twain 14

The return of Huckleberry Finn 18

Sam, Tom, and Huck 25

Huck, Pap, and the money 28

River to freedom 30

Quacks, preachers, and vagabonds 34

Robbers and runaways 41

The vanished river world 44

Final years of a modern celebrity 46

Praise and condemnation 48

Timeline 50

Further Information 52

Glossary 54

Index 56

Some words are shown in bold, **like this**. You can find out what they mean by looking in the glossary.

Sam Clemens of Hannibal, Missouri

The author of *Adventures of Huckleberry Finn*, Samuel Langhorne Clemens, is known to the world by his **pen-name**, Mark Twain. His story of the raft journey down the Mississippi River by a poor white boy Huck Finn, and his companion, the runaway black slave Jim, reflects experiences Twain had during his boyhood. Encounters along the river with robbers, murderers, feuding families, tricksters, and many others act as a background to the deepening friendship and growing trust between the two travellers. The book was a popular success from the time of its publication in 1884, and is now known as a **classic**. It is even thought by many to be the best American novel ever written.

Sam Clemens was born in 1835 in the small community of Florida in the state of Missouri. He moved with his family a few years later to the port village of Hannibal and began his life-long association with the Mississippi River. Sam Clemens' father, John, was a lawyer from Virginia and his mother, Jane, was born in Kentucky. They had four older children, but Sam was the first born in Missouri.

Sam Clemens was about fifteen years old, and working for a newspaper, when this photo was taken.

Samuel Clemens made Hannibal famous. He used it in his writing as the model for the Mississippi River town of St Petersburg, home to Huckleberry Finn and Tom Sawyer.

MARK ONE – MARK TWAIN!

Although Samuel Clemens adopted the pen-name Mark Twain, he rarely used it in his private life. "Mark Twain" was the water depth measurement used to check that river channels were deep enough for boats. Here are the depth terms used:

Mark One	1 fathom	1.8 metres (6 feet)
Mark Twain	2 fathoms	3.6 metres (12 feet)
Mark Three	3 fathoms	5.5 metres (18 feet)
Mark Four	4 fathoms	7.2 metres (24 feet)
No Bottom	5 fathoms	9.0 metres and over (more than 30 feet)

"Judge" Clemens' boy

As a professional man, John Clemens, like the doctor, the pharmacist, and the banker, had an important role to play in small town society. Appointed a **Justice of the Peace**, he was known by the honorary title of "Judge" and handed out justice in a small courtroom not far from the family home.

Hannibal had no free education for its children, but Sam Clemens' parents were wealthy enough to pay for their children to attend school. However, Sam was only eleven years old when his father suddenly became ill and died. This meant that Sam's formal schooling soon ended. The needs of the family meant he must earn money, and he started work as a printer's **apprentice**. This was the beginning of Sam Clemens' long professional connection with the printed word.

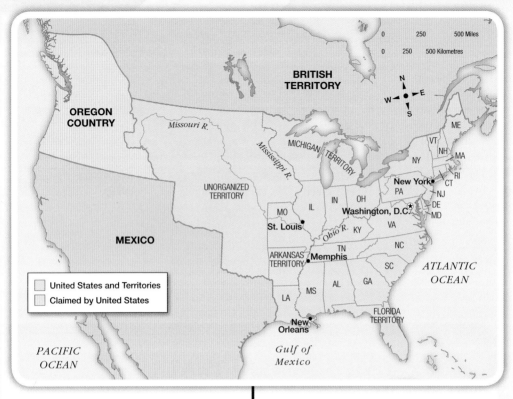

The United States in the early 1830s.

Missouri in the frontier world

In the early 1800s there was a massive movement of people to the west of the United States. The US victory against Great Britain in the **War of 1812** made new **immigrants**, as well as those already settled in the eastern states, feel it was now safe to move west. Native American nations had been defeated in the north-west and the south-west. Many of them had been forced to **cede** (give) their lands to the US government. Improved routes, such as the Cumberland Road and the Wilderness Road, and more reliable steam-powered boats made journeys west easier. Land was available after 1820 from the government for only 1.25 dollars an acre. The Clemens family's journey to Missouri was part of the great move west. Some **pioneers** were looking for religious or political freedoms. Others, like the Clemens family, were looking for economic opportunities.

The historian Frederick Jackson Turner said:

> *The rise of the new west was the most significant fact in American history in the years immediately following the War of 1812.*

Turner's views on how the American **frontier** influenced the United States' development became known as the Turner Thesis.

The Missouri problem

In the six years that followed the end of the War of 1812, six western **territories** became states. The move of the Missouri Territory to statehood was much more complicated. This was mostly because the national government was under great pressure. These all related to the question of slavery, and whether it should be allowed to expand into new areas. The Missouri Territory first asked to be made a state in 1817. At this time there were eleven **free states** and eleven **slave states**. Allowing Missouri to become a state would tip the balance – one way or the other.

The Missouri Compromise

In 1820, the US **Congress** passed the Missouri Compromise. This made the north-east state of Maine a free state and Missouri a slave state, which kept the balance between free and slave states. By the time the Clemens family settled in Missouri, it had been a slave state for nearly fifteen years and its population had rocketed. While the **census** of 1810 recorded a population of only 19,783 for the larger Missouri Territory, the result of the 1830 census for the state of Missouri was 140,455.

In 1808 the US Congress passed a law making it illegal to bring any more slaves into the United States. However, slaves already in the country could still be bought and sold in slave states. The children, grandchildren, and great-grandchildren of slaves brought from Africa before 1808 provided a continuous supply for slave dealers, like the ones shown here.

The wider world beckons

By 1853, when Sam Clemens decided to spread his wings and leave the Mississippi River valley for the wider world of the US east coast, he was a qualified **journeyman** printer. Massive growth in the printing industry meant he found it easy to get work.

Printing and the "Penny Press"

In the early 1800s there was an explosion in the quantity of material being printed. This followed the invention of the Napier steam-powered printing press, which could produce 4,000 sheets of newsprint an hour. By 1842, cheap postal rates for newspapers meant that novels were also printed like newspapers and sold by mail order for less than seven cents a copy. This forced book publishers to come out with paperback editions, as well as heavier traditional hardback books. Then, in 1847, Richard Hoe of New York invented the Hoe Rotary Press. This increased the printing rate to 20,000 printed sheets per hour.

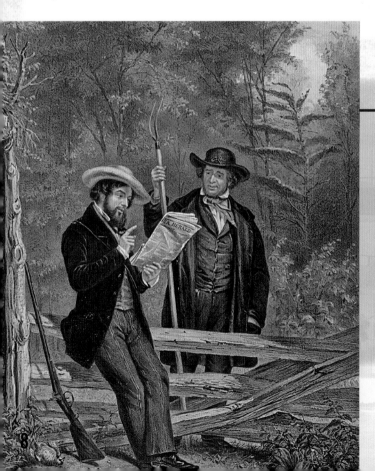

This 1853 painting by W. S. Mount, *The Herald in the Country*, showed that even in the countryside, far from the big cities, people used the New York papers to keep up with news, politics, and business.

READ ALL ABOUT IT!

The number of newspaper titles published in the United States in 1833 was 1,200. By 1860, it was 3,000. Many magazines, some aimed specifically at women such as Godey's Lady's Book, were also starting up at this time.

Horace Greeley (1811–1872) was the most influential of the pre-US Civil War newspaper editors. He had previously been a printer. Greeley started the *New York Tribune* in 1841 and edited it until his death. During his time at the *Tribune*, he campaigned for land reform, women's rights, vegetarianism, and trade unions, and against slavery and alcoholism. Greeley ran for president in 1872, but was unsuccessful.

Newspaper publishers made fortunes from these advances in technology. The number of daily newspapers – most costing only a penny a copy – multiplied. Newspapers were the main entertainment of the day, containing not only news stories, but also **sensationalist** crime, scandal, and "scoops". These were exciting new stories first printed in only one newspaper.

Popular newspapers became known as the "gutter press" because they relied on the lowest form of stories, such as gossip and scandal, often from sources that could not be trusted. In reaction, a number of new newspapers began publishing things such as book reviews and stories on **social reform** and education. The editors of these papers, such as Horace Greeley of the *New York Tribune*, James Gordon Bennett of the *New York Herald,* and Benjamin H. Day of the *New York Sun*, influenced many people's opinions.

Back to the Mississippi

Sam used his printing skills in many places during his time away from home. He later mentioned having jobs in Philadelphia, Pennsylvania, and New York City, and visiting the US capital city, Washington, D.C. In 1850, he returned to work as a printer at the newspaper owned by his older brother, Orion, in Keokuk, Iowa, up the Mississippi from Hannibal. During this time Sam first had his stories and humorous **sketches** published in local newspapers and magazines. He later wrote that by printing other writers' work he "consciously acquired what is called a [writing] style".

This photo of Sam Clemens was taken at the time he worked on the Mississippi as a river pilot.

Printing may have been his job, but Sam was never short of big ideas and dreams. Like other Americans out to earn their fortunes, he thought he would be able to trade his way to wealth. Sam set his heart on journeying up the Amazon River in South America to make his fortune, but he only got as far as heading south on a Mississippi River steamboat. A chance meeting with a river pilot who was willing to take him on as an apprentice gave Sam the opportunity to live his childhood dream.

FULL STEAM AHEAD

*By the 1850s, over 1,000 steamboats worked the Mississippi and its **tributary** rivers. The quickest ones could travel the 1,930 kilometres (1,200 miles) between the bustling river port cities of St Louis, Missouri, and New Orleans, Louisiana, in less than four days. From New Orleans, on the Gulf of Mexico, goods were sent on to the rest of the United States and the world. Entire factories, such as the Novelty Iron Works in New York, were devoted to making parts for steamboats.*

Kings of the river

Steamboat pilots, such as Horace Bixby who trained Sam Clemens, were vitally important to the use of rivers for transport and trade. By the mid-1800s, sections of railway were being built, but the river and canal systems, in particular the Mississippi River and Ohio River, were still the way most people and goods travelled.

An apprentice river pilot paid to be "taught the river" by an experienced pilot. Every obstacle, channel, and current along hundreds of miles had to be memorized. Changes in the course of the river during different seasons had to be learned. Permanent differences that came about as the result of flooding or droughts had to be remembered. By the time he became a qualified pilot, Sam knew every inch of the river that would be the focus of so much of the action in *Adventures of Huckleberry Finn*.

Moving in and out of the river ports was difficult because there was so much traffic from the many boats and ships on the Mississippi.

A nation divided against itself

Sam Clemens' time as a Mississippi River pilot showed him the importance of the river to those who lived along it. He later used many of his experiences from this time in his "river books": *The Adventures of Tom Sawyer*, *Life on the Mississippi*, and *Adventures of Huckleberry Finn*. The river brought him great joy during this period and also personal sadness. His dearly-loved younger brother Henry died in 1858 after a steamboat engine exploded. Sam had arranged Henry's job on the boat, and he always felt responsible for the death. He recalled that his brother "never did a vicious thing towards me, or towards any one else – but frequently did righteous ones". Three years later Sam himself had to give up his dream job, as civil war divided the country.

War clouds

The **Compromise of 1850** had been intended to keep the United States together, and avoid a split between free and slave states. Ten years later, no amount of compromising could maintain the **Union**. From 1854 the Kansas-Nebraska Act allowed frontier territories to vote locally for or against slavery. This meant that it was possible for slavery to spread west.

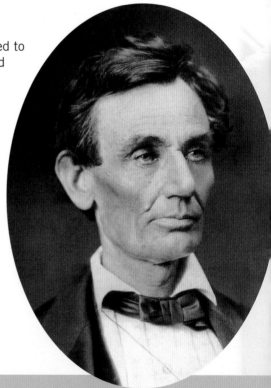

Then came the **Supreme Court's** Dred Scott Decision in 1857. The result of this was that slaves, even when freed or resident in free states, were not citizens of the United States. This meant that they were not protected by any US laws. The decision also said that laws that forbade the further spread of slavery were not legal.

During his 1858 campaign to become a **senator**, Illinois **congressman** Abraham Lincoln (above) said:

> *A house divided against itself cannot stand. I believe this government cannot endure, permanently half slave and half free.*

After John Brown and his gang were executed by hanging, he was seen as a hero of the anti-slave cause. The abolitionist poet Ralph Waldo Emerson wrote, "That new saint will make the gallows as glorious as the cross", comparing the hanging of Brown to the crucifixion of Jesus Christ.

Abolitionist anger

Those who were **abolitionists** felt betrayed. In 1859, an elderly Kansas man and his supporters took things into their own hands. John Brown was a strong Christian and **fanatically** anti-slavery. He had already carried out murders and raids into the South to free slaves. An attempt to capture the government arms depot at Harper's Ferry in West Virginia ended in defeat for Brown and his followers.

After Brown's trial and execution, public opinion was even more divided.

Abraham Lincoln, the pro-Unionist candidate, was elected president in November 1860. This made the slave states feel that their only future was in **secession** from the free states. By February 1861, seven states had broken away from the fragile Union. In mid-April 1861 the Civil War began.

Samuel Clemens wrote in 1906:

Within eighteen months I became a competent pilot, and I served that office until the Mississippi River traffic was brought to a standstill by the breaking out of the Civil War.

Mr Mark Twain

When trade was disrupted and finally stopped by the outbreak of the American Civil War in 1861, steamboat traffic on the Mississippi River ground to a halt. After piloting the last boat to get up the Mississippi before it was **blockaded**, Sam returned home to Missouri. He joined others who supported the newly formed **Confederate** States of America, which was made up of some slave states that had left the Union.

Sam's war

Missouri at the start of the war had a strong pro-Union population, even though it was a slave state. There were also many Confederate sympathizers, including the state **governor**. In an attempt to keep the state in the Union, unionist government soldiers took over land and weapons held by the governor and his pro-Confederate forces. Missouri, therefore, never left the Union for the Confederacy. Throughout the war, however, Confederate supporters, formed bands of fighters, known as raiders or bushwhackers. The most famous of these were the Anderson Gang and Quantrill's Raiders. Similar groups of Union supporters were known as jayhawkers.

Rangers, raiders, and bushwhackers

Sam, now 25 years old, became a member of a small band made up of friends from his boyhood town of Hannibal, in Marion County, Missouri. Although the group, who called themselves the Marion Rangers, were together for less than a month, for Sam it was long enough. He later remembered being warned that Union troops were coming: "This looked decidedly serious. Our boys went apart and consulted; then we went back and told the other companies present that the war was a disappointment to us and we were going to disband."

William Clarke Quantrill led the pro-Confederate bushwhackers known as Quantrill's Raiders. They attacked many civilian targets, particularly in Missouri and Kansas.

During his time out west in Nevada and California, Sam developed "Mark Twain" into a typical frontier humorist, speaking with an exaggerated southern drawl and exaggerating the facts, or telling "tall tales." Here, Twain (centre) is pictured with two friends.

Nevada Territory

Sam's short war-time experiences ended when he left the Marion Rangers. In July 1861 he headed west to the Nevada Territory with his brother Orion. Orion was a firm Union supporter, who had been appointed secretary to the territory's governor. In Nevada, the war seemed a long way away. With no need for river pilots, Sam had to turn to other jobs to make a living. He worked for his brother, and then as a **prospector**, before finally returning to the printed word.

As a printer, Sam Clemens had processed the writing of others. From as early as 1852, however, he had seen his own words in print. So, getting a job writing for the *Territorial Enterprise* newspaper in Virginia City, Nevada, was an obvious step. In Nevada and California during the next five years, now regularly using his pen-name Mark Twain, Sam gained a reputation as a humorous journalist, lecturer, and public speaker. **Commissions** for his witty and informative travel writing took him first to the Sandwich Islands (later to become the state of Hawaii) and then to Europe.

Post-war life

Union victory ended the American Civil War in the spring of 1865. The country was again under one national government, and slavery was abolished. By this time, the reputation of the writer and lecturer now known as Mark Twain had spread back to the east coast. The popularity of articles published in US newspapers during his European travels made him a recognized celebrity.

FRONTIER HUMORISTS

*The style known as frontier, or western, humour became known throughout the United States in the work of Charles Farrar Browne, who used the pen-name Artemus Ward. Other humorists with this style were David Ross Locke (known as Petroleum Nasby) and Henry Wheeler Shaw (known as Josh Billings). Browne, Locke, and Shaw created **philosopher**-type characters from backward rural areas, or "backwoods", to tell tall tales. They then performed and wrote as these characters. These comic writers, using ordinary, everyday language and spelling words as they sounded, greatly influenced Mark Twain.*

Artemus Ward (sketched here) claimed to have "discovered" Mark Twain in Nevada. Ward was an obvious influence on Twain's style as a stage lecturer, or "platform entertainer".

In 1870, Sam married Olivia Langdon. She was the sister of a wealthy companion from his trip to Europe. The couple moved to New York State. Sam was enjoying the success of the book about his travels, *Innocents Abroad*. His next book, *Roughing It*, published in 1872, was also popular. Sam was constantly in demand for lectures and after-dinner speaking. The "Mr Mark Twain" now known to the public was successful in a way that young Sam Clemens could only have dreamed about.

Olivia Langdon (1845–1904) – The lady in the portrait

Sam Clemens first saw Olivia 'Livy' Langdon in this small portrait painted on ivory that belonged to her brother, Charles. The two were married in February 1870. Throughout his career, Sam always took Livy's advice about his writing, allowing her to cut material she found too **crude** *from his work, including* Adventures of Huckleberry Finn. *In 1906 he recalled that, "Her judgements of people and things*

The return of Huckleberry Finn

In the United States' **centennial** year of 1876, *The Adventures of Tom Sawyer* by Mark Twain was published. Set in the small Mississippi River town of St Petersburg, Missouri, in the mid-1840s, it told of the exploits of Tom Sawyer, his friends, and family. One of the characters was Huckleberry Finn, a local boy the same age as the **protagonist** of the story, but with a completely different lifestyle.

While the other children in the book went to school, did chores, and were part of normal town life, Huck Finn had no structure to his existence. There was no caring family, no one to make him wash, change his clothes, or go to bed. Most of the other boys in the story thought he was the luckiest child in the world. By the end of *The Adventures of Tom Sawyer*, Huck and Tom have survived some tough scrapes and come into money. The book cried out for a sequel. Twain thought so, too, and almost immediately started working on what he at first called "Huck Finn's Autobiography".

A boy of twelve

In a letter to his friend, the author William Dean Howells in 1875, Twain wrote, "By and by I shall take a boy of twelve and run him on through life (in the **first person**) but not Tom Sawyer – He would not be a good character for it." Within the year Twain had chosen Huck as that boy and started the book that would become *Adventures of Huckleberry Finn*.

Huck Finn's home life was different from that of his comrades. Tom Sawyer found him living in a large barrel behind an abandoned slaughterhouse.

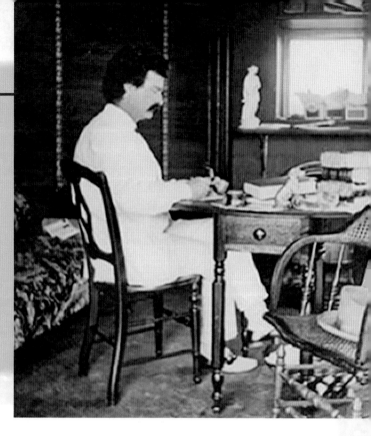

Most of *Adventures of Huckleberry Finn* was written in the summers of 1876 and 1883 at Quarry Farm, near Elmira, New York. This was the home of Livy Clemens' sister and her family. Twain liked working there in a small study.

This sequel, however, was a long time coming. Children who read and enjoyed *The Adventures of Tom Sawyer* were young adults before they could find out what happened next in St Petersburg. The first 400 handwritten pages were completed in the summer of 1876. Twain felt at the time that the book was "half-finished", but was unhappy with it and even considered burning the manuscript. Instead he put it aside for about three years before starting, bit by bit, to revise and correct the completed section of the book.

Twain wrote and published three other books while making changes to his half-finished Huck Finn story. Then, in the summer of 1883, he wrote in a letter to his brother Orion that he was "piling up manuscript in a really astonishing way". The total added up to 1,361 handwritten pages. Just over a year later, in December 1884, the first copies of *Adventures of Huckleberry Finn* were published in England. Publication in the United States followed two months later.

> *Most of the adventures recorded in this book really occurred ... Huck Finn is drawn from life ... The odd superstitions touched upon were prevalent [common] among children and slaves in the west at the period of the story - that is to say, thirty or forty years ago.*

Mark Twain in the Preface to *The Adventures of Tom Sawyer*, 1876

> **NOTICE.**
> **Persons attempting to find a Motive in this narrative will be prosecuted; persons attempting to find a Moral in it will be banished; persons attempting to find a Plot in it will be shot.**
> **By Order of the Author**
> **Per G.G. Chief of Ordnance.**

This is the humorous author's note that appears at the beginning of of all editions of *Adventures of Huckleberry Finn*.

Attempting to find a plot

In his author's note at the beginning of *Adventures of Huckleberry Finn*, Twain encourages the reader not to look for a plot – or not to take it too seriously! However, there is most certainly a story. On its most basic level the book tells of the exploits of two runaways: the escaped slave and the boy running from abusive homes and a society that they don't fit in with. Its first-person narrative makes it Huck's book, but the slave Jim and the Mississippi River itself are strong supporting characters.

Attempting to find motives and morals

Although Twain tried to deny it, there are many layers of meaning and complexities in the book. These fascinated readers, critics, and academics from the start.

One of these aspects is the use of various **dialects**, with many words spelled on the page as they sound, so the reader can say them out loud and hear how the various characters speak. In a note at the start of the book, Twain claims that in all there are seven dialects, or varieties of dialect, used. He felt it was necessary to explain this so that no reader would "suppose that all these characters were trying to talk alike and not succeeding".

Soon after the publication of *Adventures of Huckleberry Finn*, the popular author Joel Chandler Harris (see page 22) wrote to Twain, "its value as a picture of life and as a study in **philology** will come to be recognized . . . It is the most original contribution that has yet been made to American literature."

NAMED AFTER A FRUIT
– AND THE TOWN DRUNK

Huckleberries are dark blue berries that grow on low bushes, like blueberries. The name huckleberry for this type of fruit is only used in the United States. In the United Kingdom they are known as bilberries or whortleberries, sometimes spelled hortleberry. The word huckleberry probably comes from hortleberry. It became an insult meaning "common" or "stupid". The name Finn was chosen by Twain for Huckleberry, as it was the surname of one of the Hannibal town drunks of his childhood: Jimmy Finn.

Huckleberry Finn by Aloysius O'Kelly was painted in 1885, just after *Adventures of Huckleberry Finn* was published. This shows that Huck's character made an impact on readers straight away.

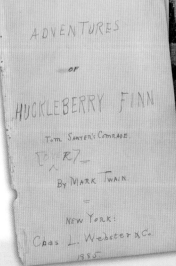

This is the title page of the original manuscript of *Adventures of Huckleberry Finn* in Twain's handwriting.

Applause and criticism

The reactions to the book were immediate and very divided. Well-known authors of the time, such as William L. Alden and William Dean Howells, thought it was the best book ever written. The famous Scottish writer Robert Louis Stevenson said it "contains many excellent things". In a letter to Twain he said he had read the book four times and was "quite ready to begin again tomorrow".

Others were negative. The Public Library of Concord, Massachusetts, removed the book from its shelves. One library member said, "It deals with a series of adventures of a very low grade of morality; it is . . . rough, ignorant dialect . . . It is also very irreverent [against religion]." The *Boston Herald* newspaper found it to be "pitched in but one key, and that is the key of a vulgar . . . life".

Joel Chandler Harris (1848–1908) was a white writer well known for writing under his pen-name, Uncle Remus. His "Brer Rabbit" and "Brer Fox" stories were written in Southern black dialect English, as if told by a black storyteller.

Edward Windsor Kemble was the illustrator for the first edition of *Adventures of Huckleberry Finn*, shown here. Twain personally chose the young cartoonist, who had published drawings in *Life* magazine and the *New York Graphic*. Twain was happy with most of the illustrations, but always thought Kemble had made Huck look too small and too young for a twelve or thirteen-year-old.

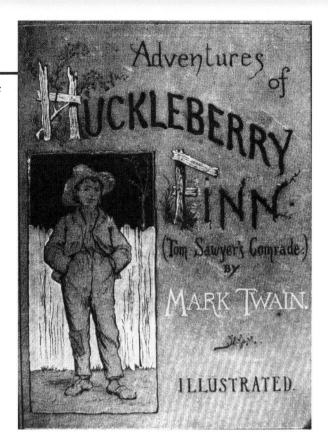

> *They [the Concord Library] have expelled Huck from their library as 'trash and suitable only for the slums'. That will sell 25,000 for us for sure.*

Mark Twain wrote this in a letter to his nephew and publishing partner, Charley Webster, at the time of the publication of *Adventures of Huckleberry Finn*.

Changing views

When it was published in the United States in 1885, none of the critics who wrote about the book commented on the word "nigger". It was used at the time to describe both slaves and free blacks. It was, however, considered to be slang, with more acceptable terms being "negro" or "coloured". But as early as 1862, the white commander of the first ex-slave regiment in the Union army, Colonel T.W. Higginson, referred to nigger as "this offensive word". Twain himself started out using the word in his first-person stories and stage lectures, but according to historian Arthur Pettit stopped using it in print when writing "as himself" in around 1869.

By 1889 the *Century Dictionary* concluded that the use of nigger "generally conveys more or less contempt". By the time the first edition of Fowler's *Modern English Usage* was published in 1926, the word was believed to show in the speaker, "if not deliberate **insolence**, at least a very arrogant inhumanity".

Twain's novel was trying to accurately recreate the language used in the mid-1840s, and the word "nigger" would have been used within the social class and normal speech of his characters. Within that specific historical context, Twain was not intending to be offensive, although the use of the word might be an example of ignorance.

> *When we consider that the programme is advertised and becomes cold-blooded newspaper reading, I think we should avoid any risk of appearing – even to the most thin-skinned ... the faintest bit gross.*

Writer George W. Cable wrote this in a letter to Mark Twain before their reading tour in 1884–1885. Cable wanted Twain to remove the word nigger from the printed programme. It referred to a reading Twain would make from *Adventures of Huckleberry Finn*.

Mark Twain (left) with George Washington Cable.

Sam, Tom, and Huck

Twain never hid the fact that the St Petersburg of the 1840s he created was really Hannibal, Missouri, where he (Sam Clemens) had grown up. In 1886, Twain went so far as to say of his Mississippi River books, "I do not know that there is any incident in them which sets itself forth as having occurred in my personal experience which did not occur."

The "real" Huck Finn once lived in this property in Hannibal, Missouri.

My mother had a good deal of trouble with me, but I think she enjoyed it. She had none at all with my brother Henry ... He is 'Sid' in Tom Sawyer. But ... Henry was a much finer and better boy than ever Sid was.

Mark Twain, 1906.

Drawn from life

If St Petersburg was Hannibal, and many of the incidents true, then were the characters in the books also drawn from life? Twain claimed that the character of Tom Sawyer was a combination of "three boys whom I knew". The most important of those boys was most certainly Sam Clemens himself. Twain kept Tom Sawyer's family close to his own. He used his mother, Jane Clemens, as the model for Tom's Aunt Polly, and his brother Henry as the inspiration for Tom's younger half-brother Sid. Tom's older cousin Mary was based on Twain's own older sister Pamela. Even the Widow Douglas had a Hannibal double in Widow Holliday, a three-times married wealthy woman who lived in a big house on Holliday Hill.

The character of Huckleberry Finn was, according to Twain, based on one individual whom anyone who "knew the Hannibal of the forties" would easily recall. Tom Blankenship was the son of one of Hannibal's town drunks, and Twain claims to have written him exactly as he really was. When he first read sections of *The Adventures of Tom Sawyer* to his family, Twain's sister Pamela said "Why that's Tom Blankenship!" when she heard Huck described.

Jane Clemens, pictured here, was the "real-life" Aunt Polly from *The Adventures of Tom Sawyer*.

> *I have drawn Tom Blankenship exactly as he was. He was ignorant, unwashed, insufficiently fed; but he had as good a heart as ever any boy had. His liberties were totally unrestricted ... and he was continuously happy, and envied by all the rest of us. As his society [friendship] was forbidden us by our parents ... we sought and got more of his society than of any other boy's.*

Mark Twain, 1906.

Hannibal was the inspiration for the small town of St Petersburg. Glasscock's Island in the river off Hannibal, now badly eroded, was the model for Jackson's Island in *The Adventures of Tom Sawyer* and *Adventures of Huckleberry Finn*.

Huck's part in Tom Sawyer's adventures ends …

At the end of *The Adventures of Tom Sawyer*, Huck Finn is a wealthy young man, having split the 12,000 dollars from the "haunted" house with Tom. Now living with the Widow Douglas, Huck has rules and regulations to follow. For a free spirit like Huck, it is almost too much to bear. He confides in Tom Sawyer, "Lookyhere Tom, being rich ain't what it's cracked up to be." The story ends with Tom convincing Huck to continue suffering the "shackles of civilization", his reward being a chance to join the yet-to-be-formed Tom Sawyer's gang of robbers.

… and his own story begins

From before he started writing Huck's story, Twain had decided it would be in the first person: in Huck's own words. So, it is from this perspective that the book starts and all of the action is told. At the beginning of the book, Huck explains that the readers won't know him unless they first read a book by Mr Mark Twain who, "told the truth, mainly. There was things which he stretched, but mainly he told the truth." The suggestion is that Huck will be a more reliable storyteller, without the intrusion of Mr Mark Twain and his stretching of the truth.

Huck, Pap, and the money

In the **backwater** of 1840s St Petersburg, the most important issues facing Huck Finn were surviving his "sivilizing" by the Widow Douglas and her sister, Miss Watson, and taking his place in Tom Sawyer's robbers' gang. However, after Huck's drunken bully of a father heard about Huck's good fortune and returned, things changed. Huck was his son, and therefore his possession, so he reasoned Huck's money rightly belonged to him.

The law of the time would have been on Pap Finn's side. As Huck relates, "[Judge Thatcher] and the widow went to law to get the court to take me away from him and let one of them be my guardian; but it was a new judge … he didn't know the old man; so he said courts musn't interfere and separate families if they could help it; said he'd druther not take a child away from its father".

The "demon drink"

Like the similar characters Twain had known in Hannibal, Pap Finn was the town drunk of St Petersburg. Frontier areas were well known for excessive drinking of alcohol, and public drunkenness was not considered a disgrace. The negative effects of drinking lots of alcohol, such as brawling, abuse within the family, and other lawlessness, led to the development of **temperance** societies. To begin with they wanted people to drink less alcohol, but eventually favoured **abstinence**: not drinking alcohol at all. Most of these societies were connected to religious organizations.

Like most "mean whites", Pap Finn was pro-slavery, anti-education, and against government interference.

WAS HUCK RICH?

The 6,000 dollars that Huck received as his part of the "haunted" house money did make him quite wealthy for the time and place, so it's not surprising that Pap Finn was willing to go to the law to get it. The equivalent to an unskilled worker today would be over a million dollars. A dollar in 1840s America was a silver coin, and ten-dollar coins were gold. Paper money did exist, but was only issued by state banks, not by the national government.

Jail was the usual punishment for drunkenness, and even the smallest towns had their own lock-up cells. Hannibal's was near Twain's childhood home, where the back of the courtroom building housed the jail. Twain's father, as a Justice of the Peace, had to deal with many drunken brawls. Like the judge in *Adventures of Huckleberry Finn* who tried to help get Pap Finn off drink, John Clemens tried to reform some of the drunks he met. He had an equal lack of success.

Backwoods "mean whites"

Pap Finn also represents a type of hard-drinking, hard-swearing character who was found at the bottom of south-west white society. Many of the unskilled jobs done by white men in the North were done by slaves in the South. This, however, did not stop white unskilled workers from being pro-slavery. Members of this type of southern underclass later became know as "poor whites" or "poor white trash", but at this time were referred to as "mean whites".

Harriet Beecher Stowe, author of *Uncle Tom's Cabin* and abolitionist said :

[Poor southern whites were] utterly ignorant and … brutal. Singular as it may appear, though slavery is the cause of the misery … of this class, yet they are … ferocious advocates [supporters] of slavery.

After Huck fakes his own death to escape from Pap, he meets up with Jim, Miss Watson's runaway slave. Jim had been Huck's friend, adviser, and **confidante** at Widow Douglas'. When they find that Jim is being sought not only as a runaway, but also as a suspect in Huck's "murder", they take off down the river together.

Jim's terror at the possibility of being "sold down to [New] Orleans" is understandable. Any healthy male slave sold down river would be likely to end up as a "field slave" on a sugar or cotton plantation. There was never any attempt made to keep slave families together, so any individual sold out of an area might never see his or her parents or children again.

This map shows the Mississippi, marked with real place names and fictional places from *Adventures of Huckleberry Finn*.

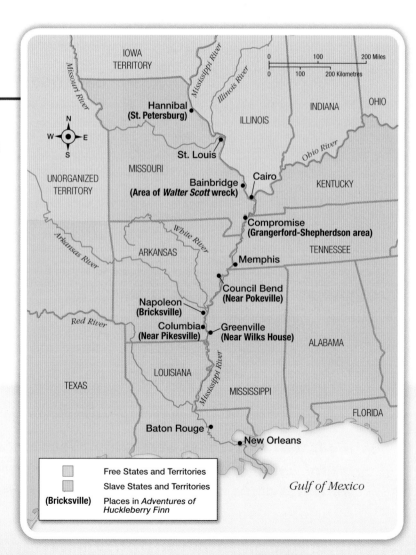

Although the state of Illinois, on the east bank of the Mississippi across from Missouri, was a free state, Jim would not have been safe landing there. Without a certificate of freedom he would have been held as an **indentured** labourer until his owner could be found to take him back.

Freedom from enslavement

Jim's goal in his river trip with Huck is to head up the Ohio River, where it runs into the Mississippi south of Cairo, Illinois. His dream destination is one of the free states up the Ohio River. From there he is unlikely to be returned to Missouri as a runaway. He could then earn money to buy his wife and children from their owner and have them join him. This was one way, full of the danger of capture and return, in which a slave could try to become free. There were other ways. Many slaves were bought and then freed by sympathetic northerners. A runaway slave could get help from an abolitionist group involved in the "underground railroad" which would help him or her escape to freedom.

At any time it was possible for an owner to free a slave. However, in slave states, such as Missouri, there were strictly enforced regulations on the movement and activities of freed slaves. Many decided to move North.

Although many people in free states were against slavery, this was not a view that all northerners held. Unskilled white labourers, especially newly-arrived immigrants, saw the free blacks in the North who worked for low wages as a threat to their jobs. This resentment exploded into violence, particularly in the large industrial northern cities. For example, in Philadelphia there were five riots against free blacks between 1832 and 1849.

"Low-down" abolitionists

When Huck first decides to join Jim, rather than turn him in as a runaway, he worries for a moment that "People will call me a low-down Ablitionist and despise me – but that don' make no difference." By showing this attitude to abolitionists, he is reflecting the accepted norm of the time in a slave state. As Twain remembered in 1895, "In those old slave-holding days the whole community was agreed as to one thing, the awful sacredness of slave property.

To help steal a horse or a cow was a low crime, but to help a hunted slave ... was a much baser crime, and carried with it a stain, a moral **smirch** which nothing could wipe away".

The first abolitionist society was set up in 1831, and by 1833 the American Anti-Slavery Society had formed. By the 1840s there was increasing support for the abolitionist cause. Amongst those who stressed that slavery was morally wrong were many members of the Society of Friends (Quakers), as well as members of other Christian **denominations**.

William Lloyd Garrison (1805–1879)

The abolitionist William Lloyd Garrison was the leading spokesman for the northern abolitionist movement. From 1831 to 1865 he was the publisher of The Liberator. *This monthly newspaper championed the abolitionist cause. It was also against capital punishment and in favour of temperance and women's rights. Garrison wrote of his firmness in the cause of the total and immediate abolition of slavery, "I will be as harsh as truth, and as uncompromising as justice."*

> **I hear ole missus tell the widder she gwyne to sell me down to Orleans, but she didn't want to, but she could git eight hund'd dollars for me, en it uz sich a big stack o' money she couldn' resis'.**
>
> Jim explains to Huck why he had to run away from his "owner" in *Adventures of Huckleberry Finn.*

The Liberator never had huge sales, but many of the articles it contained were quoted or republished in magazines or newspapers with large readerships. This made it very influential.

Head of "The Liberator."

THE "UNDERGROUND RAILROAD"

What became known as the "underground railroad" was in fact a network of safe, secret, stopping places or "safe houses" where fugitive slaves could be hidden on their way to freedom in the North. Those that helped this escape system work ranged from individuals who gave money or turned a "blind eye", to those who risked their lives. It is estimated that from the 1840s to the outbreak of the Civil War, 1,000 to 2,000 slaves a year reached freedom with the help of these safe houses.

Quacks, preachers, and vagabonds

Many of the incidents that happen, and the shady individuals Huck and Jim meet on their trip down the Mississippi are representative of real events and river types of the 1840s. During his years growing up along the river, and later working as a river pilot, Mark Twain met many colourful characters. In his autobiographical writings, he remembers the **patent medicine** sellers, travelling actors, **phrenologists**, and the **mesmerist** who came to Hannibal in his youth. Life could be filled with violence, and death was a commonplace experience. Twain saw murders, tragic accidents, and schoolmates dying young. Many families lost mothers in childbirth. Children often died of common illnesses and, in a riverside area like Hannibal, there were sometimes drownings.

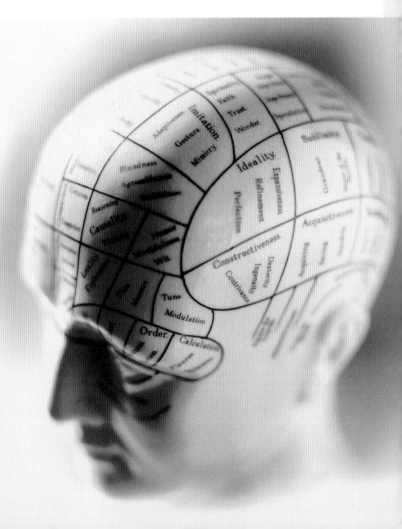

This model was used by a phrenologist. Phrenologists believed that a person's character and mental abilities could be "read" by the shape and size of their skull.

> *Miss Watson's nigger, Jim, had a hair-ball as big as your fist, which had been took out of the fourth stomach of an ox, and he used to do magic with it ... He said it would tell my whole fortune if I wanted it to.*

Huck, trying to get information about Pap from Jim's hair-ball
in *Adventures of Huckleberry Finn*.

Jim consulted the hair-ball to get answers about Huck's future.

Superstition and luck

It is not surprising that at a time when life could so easily be snuffed out that superstitions, old wives' tales, and magic were often believed in. In slave states, such as Missouri, the superstitions and belief in magic held by many slaves were added to this mix. Religious people, as represented in *Adventures of Huckleberry Finn* by Widow Douglas and Miss Watson, thought superstitions were anti-Christian and likely to lead, after death, to "the bad place" (hell).

Many times before and during their journey, Huck and Jim are influenced by common superstitions of the period. The natural world was one source of these. Huck says about accidentally killing a spider: "I didn't need anybody to tell me that that was an awful bad sign and would fetch me some bad luck." The actions of birds, snakes, and bees were also examined to see what they could say about the future.

Snake oil sellers

At a time when infectious diseases, such as scarlet fever and measles, could kill off an entire generation of children in a frontier town, parents were often desperate to find cures or potions that would prevent illness. So, as well as being superstitious, they were easy prey for dishonest medicine sellers. Most of the potions sold had no value as medicines.

Many contained high percentages of alcohol. Others had ingredients, such as snake oil, that the sellers claimed Native Americans used. The **quacks** that sold these "miracle cures" sometimes gave themselves important titles, such as professor or doctor, even though they had no qualifications.

Quack doctors, like this one, would often try to confuse and impress the people who came to listen to them. They would use complicated scientific terms that sounded good, but were as fake as the products.

Tricksters like the Duke and the King, who could turn their hands to a variety of scams, made a good living off frontier people who had little other entertainment.

As well as using fake scientific terms to impress buyers, a common technique during sales was the use of a "plant" in the audience. This person would claim to have successfully used the medicine, or would thank the "doctor" for having saved a loved one. Because there appeared to be no connection between the two, the crowd was often taken in by this type of act. The river provided an easy "highway" along which such tricksters could operate, leaving one area for another before they were found out.

KINGS AND DUKES

*The older of the two **conmen** Huck takes back to the raft claims to be the "late Dauphin" of France. In 1793 the former king of France, Louis XVI, and his queen, Marie Antoinette, were executed. Their oldest son, Louis, was about eight years old at the time of their deaths. He was known as the "Dauphin". This is the title held by the heir to the French throne. It was believed that he died in prison in 1795, but until 2000 there was no proof of this. The story told by the "Duke" about his claim to the title of Duke is loosely based on a real case known to Twain. It involved a dispute over inheritance and a large estate in the English Egerton family.*

Great awakenings

When superstition and quack medicines could not be relied upon, there was still religion. From 1800, the United States had been in the grip of a religious **revival**. It became known as the Second Great Awakening. It was called this after the Great Awakening, a time of American **evangelicalism** in the mid-1730s. The Second Great Awakening started in the New England states. It spread west where it took the form of "camp meetings". These week-long gatherings were usually held in the late summer or autumn. Participants would arrive, sometimes from quite a distance, and camp in tents, wagons, or makeshift cabins.

An 1861-1865 sketch of a prayer meeting of escaped slaves from the South, at Washington, D. C.

James McGready (c.1760-1817)

James McGready was a Presbyterian minister from the state of Pennsylvania who started Christian revivalist services in the camp meeting style. In Kentucky at the beginning of the 1800s, he began holding outdoor religious gatherings that were open to all. Others soon copied his success.

> *I have seen the person stand in one place, and jerk backward and forward in quick succession, their head nearly touching the floor behind and before. All classes, saints and sinners, the strong as well as the weak, were thus affected.*

Revivalist Barton W. Stone remembering camp meetings in the early 1800s, where people would be "overcome" with the spirit of religion.

THE CONTINUATION OF TRADITIONAL AFRICAN BELIEFS

*Slaves continued to use elements of African languages for generations. They also carried on with traditional beliefs in spirits, fortune-telling, and magic. Many slaves became Christians, particularly appreciating the idea of salvation through Jesus, and the idea of the poor inheriting the earth. Others rejected the church as an extension of the control of the white slave masters. The secret practice of traditional African religion in so-called "bush meetings" was, as one historian called it an "invisible institution of the **antebellum** South".*

Hundreds, and sometimes thousands, of people, including slaves, attended these camp meetings to hear preachers and to study the Bible. Getting involved in the services was encouraged. This could include falling to the ground in trances, jerking, crying out, and **speaking in tongues**. A travelling preacher often ran the small gatherings. Large meetings were usually **ecumenical**, including Baptists, Methodists, and Presbyterians.

Camp meetings were one of the rare times that isolated groups of settlers came together.

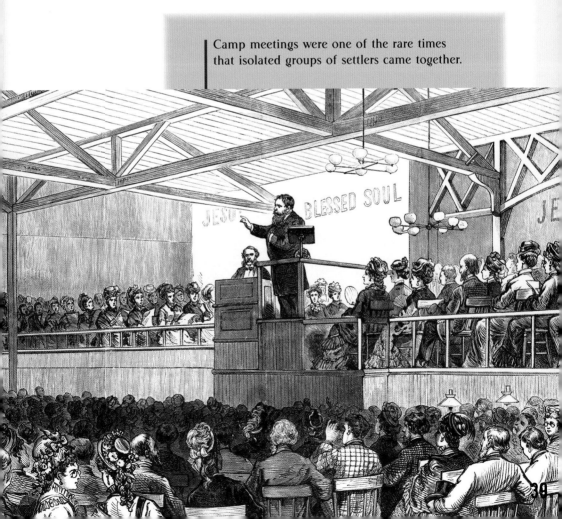

Taking the pledge

Hand in hand with the religious camp meetings were the large-scale campaigns of the temperance movement. A national body, the American Temperance Union, was set up in 1833. In 1836 it declared itself to be in favour of total abstinence from alcohol and ending the sale of alcohol. Writers, travelling speakers, and artists spoke out against the evils of "demon drink". Some states and local areas made the production and sale of alcohol illegal.

Between the 1830s and the 1860s alcohol consumption became a moral and social issue. This led to a dramatic fall in the level of excessive drinking. Many individuals pledged themselves to following the temperance cause, saying they would be **teetotal** for life.

Taking advantage

Those who genuinely practised medicine, preached religion or spoke out for the temperance cause ended up competing with **vagabonds**. These were people who pretended to be experts to win trust and con people out of their money. Perfect examples of such conmen are the characters in *Adventures of Huckleberry Finn* that become known as the Duke and the King. These rascals dabble on the dishonest side of "most anything that comes handy". As the Duke informs the King of his past adventures, "Do a little in patent medicines; theatre-actor - tragedy, you know; take a turn at mesmerism and phrenology … sling a lecture, sometimes." The King lists his specialities: "I've done considerable in the doctoring way … Preachin's my line, too; and workin' camp-meetin's; and missionaryin' around."

> *I'd been selling an article to take the tartar off the teeth - and it does take it off, too, and generly the enamel along with it - but I staid about one night longer than I ought to.*

The Duke explaining why he was being run out of town by angry customers when Huck rescued him.

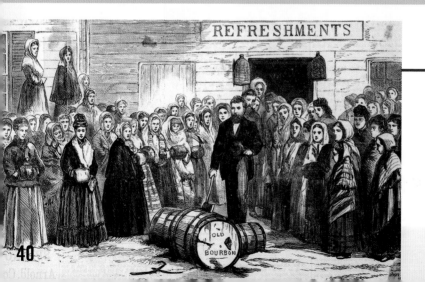

Many people who attended temperance rallies pledged themselves to living their lives without alcohol.

Robbers and runaways

Huck and Jim's time with the King and the Duke showed them some of the many ways people could be conned out of their money. It was possible to cheat the grieving and the ill. It was possible to make money by appealing to people's better nature (religious revivals), and to their worst nature (the nudity and promise of worse in the "Royal Nonesuch" performances). And, eventually, Huck and Jim themselves end up tricked, which results in capture for the runaway slave.

$150 REWARD

RANAWAY from the subscriber, on the night of the 2d instant, a negro man, who calls himself *Henry May*, about **22** years old, **5** feet **6** or **8** inches high, ordinary color, rather chunky built, bushy head, and has it divided mostly on one side, and keeps it very nicely combed; has been raised in the house, and is a first rate dining-room servant, and was in a tavern in Louisville for **18** months. I expect he is now in Louisville trying to make his escape to a free state, (in all probability to Cincinnati, Ohio.) Perhaps he may try to get employment on a steamboat. He is a good cook, and is handy in any capacity as a house servant. Had on when he left, a dark cassinett coatee, and dark striped cassinett pantaloons, new---he had other clothing. I will give **$50** reward if taken in Louisvill; **100** dollars if taken one hundred miles from Louisville in this State, and **150** dollars if taken out of this State, and delivered to me, or secured in any jail so that I can get him again. **WILLIAM BURKE.**
Bardstown, Ky., September 3d, 1838.

This handbill dates from 1838.

REWARD !

After the Duke prints the fake reward handbill so they can pretend they are returning Jim to his owner, Huck and Jim relax their guard and feel safer. This proves to have been a mistake when Jim is betrayed and sold on. Handbills like the one printed by the Duke were common, almost always showing a black man with a bundle on a stick, representing a runaway slave. There would then follow a description of the missing slave and the reward payable to anyone returning this "possession" to the rightful owner.

Free! At the end of
*Adventures of Huckleberry
Finn*, Jim finally learns of
his status as a free man,
while Huck finally learns
of his father's death.
Jim will now be able to
work to buy his wife and
children, and Huck can
"light out for the territory"
before anyone attempts
again to "sivilize" him.

Conscience

From the time that Huck decided to join Jim, he was aware of the grave risk
he was running by helping an escaping slave. On many occasions they came
near to being found out, despite running down river only at night and keeping
out of sight during the day. Up river, before they met the King and the Duke,
Huck had finally overcome the deeply-held southern morals he had been
raised to believe in. To protect Jim from the slave hunters on the **skiff**, Huck
quickly made up an elaborate lie about a family with smallpox to keep the
curious men away from the raft.

To Huck, coming up with this "dodge" was the triumph of what he saw as his
bad nature over his ability to do the right thing. He had been brought up with
certain beliefs that told him helping Jim was wrong: "Conscience says to me,
'What had poor Miss Watson done to you, that you could see her nigger go
off right under your eyes ... she tried to be good to you every way she knowed
how'." But, even though he absolutely "knowed very well I had done wrong",
Huck feels that his upbringing was wrong, and decides he will continue
helping Jim gain his freedom. Twain is purposefully **ironic** in the way he shows
Huck's decision. The reader knows that morally Huck is doing the right thing,
but Huck himself cannot escape the southern belief in slaves as valuable
property. Because of this, he sees helping the removal of that property as the
worst kind of theft.

Pirates of the Mississippi

Near the end of the book, Huck is convinced by Tom Sawyer to take part in an elaborate plan to steal back Jim from Aunt Sally Phelps' farm and escape with him. Neither Huck nor Jim know, like Tom does, that Jim is already a free man. Unlike Tom, Huck is a practical boy who has had to live on his instincts, rather than the romantic dreams and "nonsense" Tom has picked up from adventure books.

In wanting to play at, or even become, a pirate, robber, or romantic hero, Tom was suffering from the southern illness Mark Twain called "Walter Scott disease". This term refers to the influence of romantic fiction written by Scottish novelist and poet Sir Walter Scott. Twain felt that the novels of Scott could be partly blamed for the "gentlemen" of the South clinging on to what Twain called, "sham **chivalries** of a brainless and worthless long-vanished society".

Sir Walter Scott (1771–1832)

Sir Walter Scott was a widely read and popular novelist in his own lifetime. Many of his 28 books were historical novels, a style he invented and others later copied. Two of his best-known books are Rob Roy *and* Ivanhoe. *Twain admired Scott for the speed at which he wrote his books, but disliked him for reviving interest in medieval chivalry and romance*

The vanished river world

By the time *Adventures of Huckleberry Finn* was first published, in 1884, most of the riverside world and the characters that inhabited it had already disappeared into history. John Milton Hay, a native of Illinois and President Lincoln's wartime secretary, wrote to Twain soon after the book was published: "It is a strange life you have described, one which I imagine must be already pretty nearly obsolete [out of date] in most respects. I, who grew up in the midst of it, have almost forgotten it, except when I read of it in your writings - the only place, I think, where a faithful record of it survives."

Although *Adventures of Huckleberry Finn* is a record of the time in which it is set, Twain's growing unhappiness with the state of society in the late 1800s is also reflected. Attitudes towards violence, cowardice, race, religion, and money are expressed, with a **deadpan** Huck as the innocent boy recording, but not commenting on, the actions of the adults around him. This allows readers to make their own judgements about what happens.

> *The world I knew in its blossoming youth is old and bowed and melancholy now ... It will be dust and ashes when I come [here] again.*

Mark Twain wrote down his feelings about how much the Missouri of his childhood had changed in a letter to his wife, during a visit to the Mississippi Valley in 1882.

This painting by George Caleb Bingham, from around 1845, is entitled *Fur Traders Descending the Missouri*. It shows some of the river types Twain would have been familiar with in his youth. They soon disappeared from the Mississippi Valley as the frontier moved further into the "wild west".

The rail network that eventually criss-crossed the country was flexible in a way that the rivers and canals could never be.

TRIUMPH OF THE "IRON HORSE"

The westward spread of the rail network, and the rail link of the east and west coasts in 1869, changed the country. The river and canal network that had been so vital to trade, and had created jobs, a culture, and language of its own, became of less importance. Many of the riverside towns that had existed as part of this system disappeared. Hannibal was lucky in that it became a railway centre and continued to thrive until the railways themselves were overshadowed by road and air transport.

A different country

The Civil War had caused deep wounds, nationally and locally, but, in the end, had unified the country. However, the reunified country was very different from the one that had existed before the war. **Reconstruction** in the South, now without slavery, was painful and caused racial and class resentments.

In Twain's eyes, it was now a more grasping, money-hungry, and selfish nation: "All Europe and America are feverishly scrambling for money … This lust has rotted these nations; it has made them hard, sordid, ungentle, dishonest, oppressive."

Final years of a modern celebrity

In the 20 years that followed the publication of *Adventures of Huckleberry Finn*, Twain suffered bankruptcy, his wife and oldest daughter both died, and he had to cope with fame and flattery. He travelled the world and continued to write, lecture, and do book readings. He was one of the most recognizable figures in American life, and yet all this love and admiration came from a society he increasingly found himself criticizing.

For many years Twain was surrounded at his home in the east by academics and serious writers. He began to doubt the quality of his own work and no longer wanted to write "literature to please the general public", but wanted to be able to write "out of my heart, taking into account no one's feelings and no one's prejudices". It seems that Sam Clemens was getting tired of Mark Twain.

In 1902 Twain made his last visit back to Hannibal and was photographed outside his boyhood home.

> *O, Cable, I am demeaning myself - I am allowing myself to be a mere buffoon [clown]. It's ghastly. I can't endure it any longer.*

Mark Twain to fellow author and lecture circuit companion, George Washington Cable. Twain sometimes wished he could escape the character "Mark Twain, the author" that he had created and write something just to please himself.

Twain was known for his dislike of the dull, boring clothing men usually wore. Therefore he was delighted with the extravagance of the gown he had to wear to receive his honorary doctorate degree from the University of Oxford in 1907. He wore it again at the wedding of his daughter, Clara, in 1909.

BEING THE STORY AND THE STORYTELLER

Surprisingly, nearly 100 years after his death, the autobiography that Mark Twain spent so much time worrying over has never been published in full. Although a two-volume work, "Mark Twain's Autobiography", edited by Albert Bigelow Paine, was published in 1924, it contains only a fraction of the information available. Perhaps other editors are scared away by the huge quantity of material, or would rather write their own biographies of Twain.

Setting down the truth

As well as struggling with his attitudes towards his own writing, Twain was also desperate to "tell the truth" about his own life. From as early as 1870 when he was only 35, he started to set down memoirs or autobiographical notes, but was unhappy with them, always aware of holding back, or worse, exaggerating the truth. He was determined that his own life's story would not be just another Mark Twain tall tale. His last years were taken up with "the autobiography" and other writings he did not want published until after his death.

Out with the comet

The marriage and departure from home of his middle daughter, Clara, followed quickly by the death of his youngest daughter, Jean, left Twain even more bitter at the world around him. In April 1910, four months after Jean's death, Twain himself died. Samuel Clemens had started life as a weak, premature baby when Halley's Comet was making one of its periodic (every 75–76 years) appearances in the night sky. Nearly 75 years later, Twain got his wish and "went out" with the comet as it returned to the sky.

Praise and condemnation

A fact that would no doubt surprise and yet please Mark Twain, who doubted his own value and importance as a writer, is that *Adventures of Huckleberry Finn* is now one of the most popular books in American literature. It is appreciated and studied by many, from school children the age of Huck to academics in universities. It has been translated into many languages. Despite its setting in so specific a time and place, it has proved a recognizable story all around the world. US television presenter Charles Kuralt once said, "If I had to say as much about America as I possibly could in only two words, I would say . . . Huck Finn."

A "HUCKFINOMANIAC"

During his lifetime Twain had fans around the world. Irish playwright George Bernard Shaw wrote to Twain in 1907 about a conversation he had with the famous English designer William Morris. Morris had said Mark Twain was a better master of English than the more widely respected novelists Charles Dickens and W. M. Thackeray. Shaw wrote, "This delighted me extremely, as it was my own opinion; and then I found out that Morris was an incurable Huckfinomaniac."

In the 1993 film, *The Adventures of Huck Finn*, eleven-year-old Elijah Wood played Huck and Courtney B. Vance played Jim.

> *All modern American literature comes from one book by Mark Twain called* **Huckleberry Finn** *... It's the best book we've had. All American writing comes from that. There was nothing before. There has been nothing as good since.*

US novelist and Nobel Prize for Literature winner Ernest Hemingway

American actor Hal Holbrook took on Twain's lecture-tour personality for his popular one-man shows, "An Evening with Mark Twain".

Left in the past?

In the years since its publication, the novel's reputation has steadily grown, shedding the controversy about the subject matter and informal language that surrounded it in the 1880s. However, during the second half of the 1900s, there has been increased sensitivity to racist, sexist, and discriminatory language of any type in literature. *Adventures of Huckleberry Finn* has had a rocky ride. In particular it has been condemned for containing racist language, specifically the word "nigger", and some school boards and libraries have removed it from their shelves.

> *Mark Twain celebrated it [the spoken language of African Americans] in the prose of* **Huckleberry Finn;** *without the presence of blacks, the book could not have been written. No Huck and Jim, no American novel as we know it.*

African-American novelist Ralph Ellison, writing in 1970

TIMELINE

1775-1783	American War of Independence.
1803	Louisiana Purchase by US from France of territory west of the Mississippi.
1808	African slave trade banned by the US congress from 1 January, outlawing further importation of slaves into any territory in the control of the United States.
1812 -1815	War of 1812 between the United Sates and Great Britain.
1819	Hannibal, Missouri is founded by Moses Bates.
1820	Missouri Compromise passed.
1821	Missouri becomes the 24th state of the United States of America.
1823	John Clemens marries Jane Lampton.
1831	First issue of abolitionist magazine, *The Liberator*, is published.
1834	John Clemens, his wife and four children settle in Florida, Missouri.
1835	(30 November) Samuel Langhorne Clemens born.
1839	Clemens family moves to Hannibal, Missouri.
1846-1848	Mexican War.
1847	John Clemens dies.
1848	Sam leaves school to work for a printer.
1850	Compromise of 1850, five bills passed that postpone a showdown over slavery. These included the Fugitive Slave Act.
1852-1856	Sam's first sketches and stories are published in newspapers and magazines.
1853	Sam travels to the US east coast and works various jobs in the printing trade.
1854	Kansas-Nebraska Act signed.
1857	The Dred Scott Decision given by the Supreme Court.
1857	Sam starts his apprenticeship as a Mississippi riverboat pilot.
1859	John Brown's raid on the US military arsenal in Virginia.
1861-1865	American Civil War.
1861	Sam goes west to Nevada with his brother, Orion.

KEY	World history
	Local/national history (USA)
	Author's life
	Adventures of Huckleberry Finn

1862	Emancipation Proclamation signed by President Lincoln which states that on 1 January 1863 all slaves living in territories in rebellion will be declared forever free.
1865	Thirteenth Amendment to the US Constitution, prohibiting slavery, is adopted after being passed by two-thirds of the states.
1865	President Abraham Lincoln is assassinated on April 15.
1862-66	Sam works as a newspaper journalist in Nevada and California.
1866	Sam first takes to the lecture stage as Mr Mark Twain.
1868	General Ulysses S. Grant is elected President of the United States.
1870	Sam marries Olivia Langdon.
1871	Sam Clemens and his wife and son move from New York to Connecticut.
1872	Son Langdon dies of diphtheria, aged 19 months.
1872	Grant is elected to a second term as president.
1876	*The Adventures of Tom Sawyer* is published.
1884	*Adventures of Huckleberry Finn* is published in the United Kingdom in December.
1885	*Adventures of Huckleberry Finn* is published in the United States on 18 February.
1894	Business failures leave Samuel Clemens bankrupt.
1896	Daughter Susie dies of meningitis, aged 24.
1904	Wife Olivia dies in Italy.
1907	Samuel Clemens is awarded an honorary doctorate degree by the University of Oxford.
1909	Daughter Jean dies after years of ill-health, aged 29.
1910	(21 April) Samuel Langhorne Clemens dies, aged 74.
1914-1918	World War I.
1939-1945	World War II.
1962	Last surviving child, daughter Clara, dies.
1966	Sam's only grandchild, Clara's daughter Nina Galbrilowitsch, dies, ending the family line.

FURTHER INFORMATION

Other works by Mark Twain

The Celebrated Jumping Frog of Calaveras County and Other Sketches (1867)
Innocents Abroad (1869)
Roughing It (1872)
The Gilded Age [with Charles Dudley Warner] (1873)
The Adventures of Tom Sawyer (1876)
A Tramp Abroad (1880)
The Prince and the Pauper (1881)
Life on the Mississippi (1883)
A Connecticut Yankee in King Arthur's Court (1889)
The Tragedy of Pudd'nhead Wilson (1894)
Tom Sawyer, Detective (1896)
The Man Who Corrupted Hadleyburg (1899)
The Mysterious Stranger (1916)

Books about Mark Twain, and Slavery

Bial, Raymond, *The Underground Railroad* (Houghton Mifflin, 1999)
Hamilton, Virginia et al, *Many Thousand Gone: African Americans from Slavery to Freedom* (Knopf, 1993)
Middleton, Haydn, *Mark Twain* (Heinemann Library, 2001)
Miller, William, *Frederick Douglass: The Last Days of Slavery* (Sagebrush Bound, 1999)
Powers, Ron, *Mark Twain: a life* (Scribner, 2006)

Twain websites

www.42explore.com/twain.htm
This site has lots of links to useful information about Mark Twain.
www.marktwainhouse.org
A site all about the museum now in Mark Twain's house.
www.twainquotes.com
Find quotes, pictures, and interesting information related to Mark Twain.

Places to visit or contact

In the United States, there are four main locations you can visit to find out more about Samuel Clemens and the books he wrote under the name Mark Twain:

Mark Twain Birthplace State Historic Site, 37352 Shrine Road, Florida, Missouri 65283. For opening hours call 573-565-3449.

Mark Twain Boyhood Home and Museum Complex, 120 North Main Street, Hannibal, Missouri 63401. For opening hours call 573-221-9010. This complex of historic sites, museums, and interpretative centres includes the home of Sam Clemens' boyhood friend Tom Blankenship, his inspiration for the character of Huck Finn.

Mark Twain Cave, Highway 79, one mile south of Hannibal, PO Box 913, Hannibal, Missouri 63401. For opening hours call 573-221-1656. The cave now known as the Mark Twain Cave was frequently visited from the time of its discovery in the early 19th century and is an important feature in *The Adventures of Tom Sawyer*.

Elmira College Center for Mark Twain Studies. *Adventures of Huckleberry Finn* was started in 1876 and completed in 1883 at Quarry Farm near Elmira, the home of the Cranes, Olivia Clemens' sister and brother-in-law. For more information visit www.twaincenter@elmira.edu.

Films

The Adventures of Mark Twain (1985)
Directed by Will Vinton and starring James Whitmore and Carol Edelman.
Mark Twain (2001)
Directed by Ken Burns.
The Adventures of Huck Finn (1993)
A Disney film directed by Stephen Sommers, starring Elijah Wood and Courtney B. Vance.
The Adventures of Tom Sawyer (1938)
Directed by Norman Taurog and starring Tommy Kelly and Ann Gillis.

GLOSSARY

abolitionism movement that campaigned for the end, or abolishing, of slavery. Supporters were known as abolitionists.

abstinence never doing something. Abstinence from alcohol means never drinking alcohol.

antebellum existing before a certain war

apprentice someone who learns a trade by working with a skilled person

backwater place that is isolated or considered insignificant

blockade stopping access, usually by putting up barriers

cede give up or surrender something to someone else

census official count of the population

centennial marking the end of 100 years

chivalry system of qualities and customs of medieval knighthood

classic work of literature recognized over many years as being excellent

commission being employed to perform a particular task, such as writing a specific story

Compromise of 1850 five bills that postponed reforms over slavery

Confederate supporter of the southern states that formed the Confederate States of America

confidante someone confided in

Congress two elected representative bodies that form the law-making branch of the US government. The two parts are called the Senate and the House of representatives.

congressman person elected by a state to serve in the House of Representatives, part of the US Congress

conman person who cheats or swindles others after gaining their confidence and trust

crude vulgar

deadpan serious or detached manner

denomination Christian group

dialect variety of a language spoken by people from a particular social group or geographical area

ecumenical including all Christian denominations

evangelicalism preaching of the Christian gospel with emphasis on personal experience

fanatical having an extreme interest or enthusiasm for something

first person where a character tells, or narrates, the story, using "I"

free state state where owning slaves was not allowed

frontier land that is at the furthest edge of a country's settled territory

governor elected leader of the state government in a US state

immigrant someone who leaves his or her country of birth for a new life in another country

indentured legally bound to work for someone

insolence bold disrespect

ironic using irony. Words that say the opposite of what is meant.

journeyman person who has served an apprenticeship in an occupation and is qualified to do this work under someone else

Justice of the Peace appointed public official who can try some civil and criminal legal cases, administer oaths and solemnize marriages

mesmerist hypnotist

patent medicine non-prescription drug the formula of which is owned by the person or company that made it

pen-name false name used by a writer

philology study of words and language

philosopher person who offers views on important questions in life

phrenologist someone who claimed to be able to diagnose diseases or predict future problems by feeling bumps on a person's head

pioneers first people to settle in a region opening it up for development

prospector someone who searches for valuable metals or gemstones

protagonist leading character in a play or book

quack someone who pretends to have medical skill or knowledge

Reconstruction the rebuilding and renewal of the South after the American Civil War

revival reawakening of interest or acceptance of something

secession withdrawal from something

senator person elected to serve in the Senate, part of the US Congress

sensationalist something intended to surprise or create emotional excitement

sketch short, usually comic, piece of descriptive writing

skiff small open boat

slave state state where white people were allowed to own black people and make them work as slaves. Children born to slaves in these states were also slaves and the property of whoever owned their parents. Slaves could be bought and sold, as if they were a livestock.

smirch dirty mark, stain, or smear

social reform change intended to improve society

speaking in tongues talking in a language that no one can understand while in a religious trance

Supreme Court highest court in the US justice system

teetotal never drinks alcohol

temperance avoidance of alcohol

territory an organized division of a country without the full rights of a state

tributary stream or small river that flows into a bigger river

Union union of all the states of the United States as one country, with the same national government. Supporters of the Union were known as unionists.

vagabond someone who wanders from place to place

War of 1812 conflict on US soil that lasted for two years between the United States on one side, and Great Britain and its Native American allies on the other

INDEX

abolitionists 13, 31, 32
*Adventures of Huckleberry
Finn* 17–30
adaptation 48
character sources 25–26
critical reception 20, 22,
23, 48
dialects 20
narrator 20, 27
storyline 20
style and themes 4, 11,
28–43, 44
*Adventures of Tom
Sawyer, The* 12, 18, 19,
24, 27
alcoholism 9, 28, 29
Alden, William L. 22
American Civil War 12,
13-15, 16, 45

Bennett, James Gordon 9
Bingham, George Caleb 44
Bixby, Horace 11
Blankenship, Tom 25, 26
Brown, John 13
Browne, Charles Farrar
(Artemus Ward) 16
bushwackers 14

Cable, George W. 24, 46
camp meetings 38, 39
Clemens, Samuel see
Twain, Mark

Dauphin of France 37
Day, Benjamin H. 9
dialects 20
Dred Scott Decision 12

Ellison, Ralph 49
Emerson, Ralph Waldo 13
evangelicanism 38

frontier humorists 15, 16, 17
frontier thesis 6

Garrison, William Lloyd 32
Greeley, Horace 9

handbills 41

Hannibal 4, 5, 14, 24, 25,
26, 29, 34, 45, 46
Harris, Joel Chandler 20, 22
Hay, John Milton 44
Hemingway, Ernest 49
Holbrook, Hal 49
Howells, William Dean 18, 22
huckleberries 21

irony 42

jayhawkers 14

Kansas-Nebraska Act 12
Kemble, Edward Windsor 23
Kuralt, Charles 48

Langdon, Olivia 17
Liberator 32, 33
Life on the Mississippi 11,
12
Lincoln, Abraham 12, 13
Locke, David Ross (Petroleum
Nasby) 16

McGready, James 38
magic and superstition 35,
39
mesmerism 34
Missouri 4, 6, 7, 14, 31,
35, 44
Missouri Compromise 7, 12
Morris, William 48
Mount, W.S. 8

Native Americans 6, 36
newspapers 8, 9, 32, 33

phrenologists 34
pioneers 6
"poor whites" 28, 29, 31
printing industry 8-9

quack medicines 36-37
Quantrill's Raiders 14

racist language 23–24, 49
railways 45
Reconstruction 45

religious revival 38–39
river and canal network 10,
11, 45
romantic fiction 43

Scott, Sir Walter 43
Second Great Awakening 38
Shaw, George Bernard 48
Shaw, Henry Wheeler (Josh
Billings) 16
slavery 7, 9, 12, 16, 23,
29, 30
abolitionists 13, 31, 32
free blacks 23, 31, 42
fugitive slaves 31, 33, 41,
42
slave religious practices 39
social change 44-45
steamboats 10–11
Stevenson, Robert Louis 22
Stowe, Harriet Beecher 29

temperance movement 28,
32, 40
tricksters 37, 40, 41
Turner, Frederick Jackson 6
Twain, Mark (Samuel
Langhorne Clemens)
autobiographical writings
34, 47
celebrity status 16, 46
early life 4-11
lecture tours/public
readings 16, 17, 24
marriage and family 17,
46, 47
pen-name 4, 5
printing occupation 4, 5,
8, 10, 15
river pilot 10–11, 12, 13,
14
wartime experiences 14–15
writing career 10, 15, 17

"underground railroad" 31,
33

Titles in the *History in Literature* series include:

Hardback   0 431 08137 3

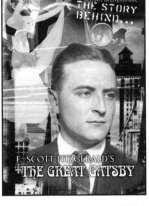

Hardback   0 431 08170 0

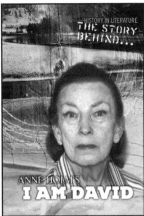

Hardback   0 431 08169 7

Hardback   0 431 08173 5

Hardback   0 431 08168 9

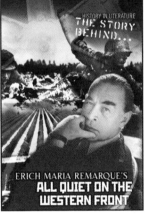

Hardback   0 431 08175 1

Hardback   0 431 08172 7

Hardback   0 431 08171 9

Find out about other titles from Heinemann Library on our website www.heinemann.co.uk/library